# NEW BEGINNINGS

# NEW BEGINNINGS

## WHEN THE MORNING COMES:

## POETRY FOR A NEW DAY

RENARD PRESS

RENARD PRESS LTD

Kemp House
152–160 City Road
London EC1V 2NX
United Kingdom
info@renardpress.com
020 8050 2928

www.renardpress.com

*New Beginnings* first published by Renard Press Ltd in 2021



Cover design by Will Dady

Printed in the United Kingdom by Severn

Paperback ISBN: 978-1-913724-45-0
eBook ISBN: 978-1-913724-62-7

9 8 7 6 5 4 3 2 1

# CONTENTS

# ABOUT NEW BEGINNINGS

In February 2021 Renard put out a call for submissions for the New Beginnings poetry project, a competition open to all those who 'felt their voice was silenced in 2020', no matter where they were in the world, or what age. The book you're holding is the result, containing all of the poems on the shortlist, and is a celebration of the end of many of the toxic aspects of 2020 and the Covid pandemic we all lived through, and offers a glimmer of hope for the future and a manifesto for change.

As with any project, there were several vital people working away behind the scenes. The judges – Miriam Halahmy, Denise Rawls, Hannah Fields and Tom Denbigh – had the unenviable task of whittling down a vast pile of submissions to the shortlist you see here today, and it is testament to their skill and patience that the list is so varied and rich in talent.

The project was supported by a crowdfunding campaign, the kind contributions to which paid for the prizes and rewards – thanks in abundance go to all those who supported the project, and their names can be found on p 122.

Thanks must also go to Ruth Irwin, Matt Dady-Leonard and Finn Dady for their suggestions and input, without which this project might never have come to fruition.

THE PUBLISHER

# ABOUT THE JUDGES

MIRIAM HALAHMY

Miriam was a teacher for 25 years, and, having worked with refugees and asylum seekers in schools, her writing engages with historical and contemporary issues that affect children across time – most notably the plight of refugees. Her young-adult novel, *Hidden*, was a *Sunday Times* Children's Book of the Week, was nominated for the Carnegie Medal and has been adapted for the stage. *Saving Hanno*, her latest book, is about a boy who comes to the UK on the Kindertransport, and reflects on the grief and loss experienced by refugee children.

DENISE RAWLS

Denise is a writer, based in east London. She is an alumni of Spread the Word's Development Programme; the first chapters of her novel in progress achieved 'highly commended' in the Writers & Artists Working-Class Writers' Prize; and she is contributing to *Common Gossip*, a working-class anthology. Outside of writing, she has been vocal about the lack of career progression across the civil service for black and brown women on BBC's *Women's Hour* and Sky News. As well as writing her novel, *Marisol's Baby*, Denise works for the National Theatre, where she leads the organisation's communications team.

HANNAH FIELDS

Hannah is a writer, editor and publisher from Texas. She founded the independent publishing company, Folkways Press, in 2020, and launched the company with an anthology, *We Are Not Shadows*, as its inaugural publication. The anthology selected writing from women of all ages and backgrounds and covers a wide range of topics – including issues of race, gender, sexuality, trauma, adversity, disability, and more. She has worked on various publications, from children's books to award-winning magazines, along with various publishers in the US and UK.

TOM DENBIGH

Tom lives in Bristol with an obscene number of books. He is the first Bristol Pride Poet Laureate and a BBC 1Extra Emerging Artist Talent Search winner. He has performed at the Royal Albert Hall and festivals around the UK, and has brought poetry to Brighton and London Pride. He is a producer at Milk Poetry and has facilitated writing workshops for groups of students from the UK and abroad. He is particularly proud of his work with queer young people. His debut collection *...and then she ate him* is out now with Burning Eye Books.

# NEW BEGINNINGS

### WINNER

UNIVERSITY WILL BE ONLINE TODAY

*Martha Grogan*

### RUNNER-UP

TODAY WE ARE ALLOWED TO HUG AGAIN

*Rosie Gliddon*

## SPECIAL MENTIONS FROM THE JUDGES

### MIRIAM HALAHMY

SICK RAPUNZEL

*Charlotte Murray*

### DENISE RAWLS

GOD ONLY KNOWS THE BLEND

*Ellie Herda-Grimwood*

### HANNAH FIELDS

THE RACE

*Oyinmiebi Youdeowei*

### TOM DENBIGH

FOUR WEEKS

*Allie Bullivant*

# UNIVERSITY WILL BE ONLINE TODAY

*Martha Grogan*

I write essays on queer literature
As you stream games from last year.
You decode a cipher a page and let
Me watch as I knit over the Internet.

University will be online this week.

You leave tupperware meals on my doormat,
Bao buns, katsu curry and pulled pork with all the fat.
I eat them in bed, tucking pillows around me,
And imagine they're your arms in a brushed cotton sea.

University will be online this month.

My mum wants to know your address for a task,
To post you a new-sewn mask
With three layers and fabric adorned with chickens,
And a nose clip to stop the fog on your glasses' lens.

University will be online this term.

Park-crossed lovers, standing in the rain,
The gardens are empty between the river and cobbled lane.
We bring our own coffee in flasks.
We hide under umbrellas, and smile six feet apart.

University will be online this year.

The closest I have come to being kissed
Was when my lateral flow test missed
My throat landed on my tongue.
The nurses' praises were coughed, not sung.

University will be online.

# TODAY WE ARE ALLOWED TO HUG AGAIN

*Rosie Gliddon*

Today we are allowed to hug again,
And yet you are no longer here to hold.
I see people, warm in their embrace
Whilst I stand alone and cold.

After two cancelled weddings in 2020,
It was hard to be positive, any more.
Next year will be a better year, they said,
Your luck will change for sure.

The first one was an easy decision,
Cancelled months in advance.
When we rebooked it for later in the year
I felt we really had a chance.

Alas, lockdown closed our doors again.
Plant the flowers back in the dirt,
Hang the dress back in the cupboard,
Try to best hide the hurt.

It will happen some day! Just be patient,
Came the usual consolation prize.
I'd smile and nod, knowing then it would.
Now, holding back tears in my eyes

It's easier to pretend it's still 2020,
The year we were so desperate to end.
You were still here, we were so happy
And now I've lost my best friend.

It was quick and painless, I'm told.
Barely forty days into this great new year.
You couldn't hear me say goodbye
As I watched you disappear.

I held your hand as tight as I could,
Wishing for this not to be true.
Insides shattered, razor-sharp pain.
How can I live without you?

So, as restrictions are eased,
My sky is for ever grey.
No one dares ask the question,
When is the big day?

# 270,000,000

*Melissa Sia*

What if my roots are in China?
Heartbeat red,
complexion fast,
skin scaled,
a celebration of peace,
the masculine and the feminine.

To survive at all costs,
to survive even though it hurts,
to survive
after
the ringing.

I am compact,
heartbeat read,
read me – not dead.

A wishing well,
copper coins,
I was stretched
across green expanses.
Large space;
silent escape.

When I was five,
my mother told me that people
die
because they are too perfect
for a world so sour.
But does that mean everyone
living
is flawed?
Mouths stitched shut.
Eyes wide open.
    Tethered,
        tethered,
            tethered.

In a parallel universe
it was a full moon.

In a parallel universe
I slept till noon.

When I was eleven,
my father told me to hit
back
if I am hurt.

But what if it hurt
too much
for my mind to process?

What if the pain isn't physical?

## 270,000,000

In a parallel universe
I am Gingko biloba,
with my antique brass arms
jutting out
with fine veins.

I chose my first kiss
with you
to be cotton
on cotton
on cotton.

You are a field of trees,
and I am anchored
            (a root).

# A COUNTRYSIDE WALK

*Heather Rodgers*

It is raining again
I turn my map over, hunching to shield those delicate
pages as I squint for the green line
The dog barks as a tractor passes and petrichor mixes
with freshly spread dung
I breathe in

Raindrops and heavy sunlight mingle on my eyelids
in an act of defiance
The ground squelches under my wellies and old
pebbles churn in fresh graves
Grass seeds beneath beginning to crack

I am alternately sinking and striding as I cross
furrowed rows, still water yielding to new life
The next ditch I stumble over is easily cleared by my
four-legged companion
Though she is not well-trained
My shoulder aches two miles in, but we are smiling
anyway
As a butterfly crosses our path, chasing whispers
through mist-laden air

There are warning signs ahead
Rabbit holes across private land and electric fences surrounding nervous horses
(Fear sets her muscles solid and I think I am the nervous one)
Berries catch in my hair and bushes scratch at my hands
As we jump yet another stile that rotted long ago

I have to circle around an unmarked pond twice; this land has shifted over time
But the hills have not
And the countryside is in our bones
Even if it is the roar of traffic that guides me onwards

I breathe in

The mud flakes off my clothes,
Pages rustle in barely-there wind
And that carefully pencilled line behind us
Etches over
Beneath a changing sky

# A NEW DAY

*Laura Chouette*

All I ask the new day for
Is to fall silently into the spaces
That the last one left empty.
Filling them with a hope
That tells me gently at dawn
That my simple love can cure
Even the most extraordinary heart,
And that my broken past
Is enough for each tomorrow that follows.
Maybe it will even remind me
That all the mistakes
I will collect tomorrow
Are not as bad
As the chances missed today.

# AFFECTION IN THE TIME OF COVID

*Lizzy Lister*

We are all weapons now,
Oblivious to whether the fuse is lit
Or the detonator is dud –

So we keep our distance;
The air a peril of maybe-germs,
An invisible war of attrition.

We juggle odds against a chalice of future guilt.
Could I live with hurting you?
Which is the tightest noose – disease or loneliness?

On the phone your voice is too far away.
How are you? How's your chest?
Did you plant the walnuts?

An awkward finish.
See you soon. I'll call tomorrow.
Lots of love.

When you stand in the doorway
I do not come close. We do not touch.

We are all weapons now,
Lining our wake with collateral damage,
Oblivious to whether the fuse is lit
Or the detonator is dud.

# AFTER LOCKDOWN, I'M QUICKER OFF THE MARK

*Catherine Edmunds*

A guitar
propped in the corner of the charity shop
like a magnet.
I must have it.
Don't care if it's rubbish.
Whenever I see guitars in charity shops
I dither,
go back the next day and they're gone.
Not today.

Two other women in the shop –
I veer round the T-shirts and trousers,
overtake them,
arrive at the guitar.

It's fully strung.
I stroke the strings.
They work.

Good enough for me.
Pick it up, check the price
(twelve quid).

Can't see any cracks.
Take it straight to the till,
straight home.

Tuners won't turn.
Out comes the WD40.
Tuners turn.

But string doesn't change pitch.
Eh? Why not?
Because the last person to string this instrument
got them topsy turvy.

No matter.
Easily sorted,
easily tuned.

Against all the odds
it sounds lovely.
It is the most beautiful sound I've heard
since before lockdown –
even longer than that.

How can it be so beautiful,
this tatty old guitar?
How can I have forgotten
so much beauty?

# ALARM IN THE CCU

*Heinrich Beindorf*

Mine were different days, I say –
all coffee without milk
travel without fear
cigs without filter
seats without belts
love without condoms
beginnings without end
the best…

easy now, she warns
checking my IVs
fiddling with the cardiac monitor
a pale chica who longboards to work
slim tattooed iPodded vegan
it's wot got you 'ere, innit

and I wince defiantly
sparking LEDs & blip salvos
ever flush with golden echoes
of books & beaches, blondes & T-Birds
all one's own bright tomorrows
so off and rapacious now
with that austere future looming
and now ours to share for cause

so thankoo, Doc, I mutter and
she pats me on the elbow

thus the baton is passed
across
the divide.

## BECOMING

*Simon Jackson*

I am secret
I am your secret
hidden even to you

a twinkle inside
planted roughly in your galaxy
a star's reflection in warm salt sea

this clumsy grapple
this tangle of limbs
this fumble of falling clothing

this hungry suckling
these greedy mouths joining
this hot panting

moaning like wounded animals
this seed of new beginning
is this love?

I am unexpected
still unknown
something shocking

you will know me first
as a sickness then a hunger
and a slow swelling

all I know is this warm sea
this lifeline anchoring me
to your heartbeat

I am adrift in a capsule
round as the moon
pulling the tides behind me

I travel hopefully trusting my line
will hold firm until arrival
one cord stretching to the curved sail

a billowing spinnaker before me
a gentle thunder pulsing around
like breaking waves the surge of surf

I am the piece of grit
hoping to become a pearl

## CHASING RAINBOWS

*Lucy Beckley*

And so it becomes the smallest of things,
The everyday,
Droplets of joy,
Squeezed out of the most mundane.
Voices may rise
And tempers will flare,
Time will stretch,
And slow,
As walls crowd in.

The path ahead unworn,
Unknown.
But I look to the moment of coming together again
With renewed sight.

When the sun
Is the most welcome, warm embrace,
The sound of rain,
A refreshing refrain,
Permeates the stale.

The freedom to walk
In the open air,
Within fingertip touching
Hip brushing distance.

The chance
To chase the rainbows,
To laugh,
To run.

To unmask the frown,
Turn it into a crown,
Of everyday ordinary joy,
Worn with pride.

The simplest of pleasures –
A kiss,
A soft hand squish –
I savour them now,
For ever more.

# DENOUEMENT

*Lynne Taylor*

When the future begins
It will be somewhere elevated,
With a muted view of busyness.

There will be hues:
Victorian Lace,
Almond Haze, Vanilla;

Soft sofas jewelled
With cushions of ochre,
Saffron, harvest gold.

Deep carpets,
Or maybe wooden floors
With tapestried rugs.

Windows on two sides;
Huge mirrors on the others,
To give weight to the light.

Time will be suspended
In filigree frames on silver chains,
Arranged in a random mosaic.

It will be a place to muse
On selves that might have been;
That may still be.

And flowers: freesias, sweet peas,
Roses; the room alive
With the sap-green scent of them.

If ever there are thorns,
There will be the salve
Of Bach's cello concerto.

It will be like
Entering a garden
After a storm.

# DYSPHORIA

*Kay Saunders*

He sits there, across from me.
Sprawled over the armchair, legs at five to three.
He is *me*, but
Different.
He likes to read, he likes to write,
He places his crystals on the windowsill at night.
He layers his jewellery and stacks his rings;
His shelves are full, full to the brim;
He doesn't like people touching his things.
He likes magnets and stickers and things made of clay;
He likes teapots and guitar picks, even though he can't play;
He likes empty notebooks and looking at the stars;
He never knows how far is too far;
He likes soft things and soft toys, but
He is a boy.
And I am not a boy.

His hair covers his brows – one slit, impulsively, in the
bathroom one evening –
And it curls, mostly at the ends.
He's pale, not porcelain;
His skin is textured and splotched
And runs in a jagged line down,
Down

Over the bump in his throat that I don't have,
And the flat chest that
Allows him to lay on his front comfortably,
And a bumpless stomach not holding the organ I do have.

He walks with size nines and holds with
Hands larger than mine with fingers longer than mine;
He is broad but lean, and goes running at night;
He uses glass water bottles not plastic;
He drops coins in donation boxes;
He watches the news;
He strokes cats in the street;
He is me, so painfully me –
So me that if I touch him I'm sure we would melt –
And yet,
He is a boy.
And I am not a boy.

I am told that because I am not a boy –
Because I am a girl –
My legs cannot be sprawled,
My skin should be porcelain,
I cannot go running at night.

I did not sit right in my own skin. I
Was too big,
Too long,
Too masculine,
And that was wrong.
But,

I like to read,
I like to write,
I place my crystals on the windowsill at night.
I layer my jewellery and stack my rings;
My shelves are full, full to the brim;
I don't like people touching my things;
I like magnets and stickers and things made of clay;
I like teapots and guitar picks, even though I can't play;
I like empty notebooks and looking at the stars;
I never know how far is too far;
I like soft things and soft toys, and
I feel like a boy.

And maybe that's all right.

## FOUR WEEKS

*Allie Bullivant*

One evening last spring
Your father and I scattered
A handful of poppy seeds
Into the tall arms
Of a meadow. Bedford,
Light slanted pink
On a tuft of snowdrops
And the belly of a bunny,
A cotton-streak under
Reeds. We expected little
To come of this gesture,
The somewhat idle hope
For a wildflower
To find purchase
Despite the rough rule
Of nature. We returned
A month later: no sign.
Still, I remember
How they tickled my palm,
Grains that could have
Fallen from a slice of bread
When I cast them
Into indifferent dusk.

Now as you burrow,
Four weeks along,
I like to picture the oak
In the centre of that meadow,
The hum of river
And mossy bank, shimmer
Of a fish growing sharper
Near the surface,
Like a face that starts
To form, slicked over
With break of water,
Shatter of a first cry.

# GETTING A VOICE BACK

*John Gallas*

*'There is always room for kindness.'*
CROATIAN PROVERB

Rosa Horvat's hound attacked my legs.
I couldn't talk. I had a dizzy fit.
They took me to the hospital in Split.
The wards were full and shut. So Uncle Dregs
Sat by my trolley till he went to work,
Then Erno, who's my mum's half-brother's son,
Pushed me up and down the hall for fun,
Before his granddad's nephew, who's a Turk,
Came and told me jokes. I nodded off.
I woke all sweaty. Sitting on my bed
Was someone with a helmet on her head.
The plastic visor shone. She had a cough.
'You'll be fine', she said. And it was true.
I found my voice. I hope she went home too.

# GOD ONLY KNOWS THE BLEND

*Ellie Herda-Grimwood*

I didn't say goodbye to you,
like I always thought I could.
Wasn't there to sit with you,
like I always knew I would.

Couldn't hold your hand
when you tried to stand
and your wise eyes scanned
the empty room unmanned.
This pandemic
was altogether unplanned,
and I hope you understand
in the end,
that I'd have been there if I could,
in the end.

I'd never have left you to fend
by yourself,
alone to wind and wend.
I would have tended
and mended
and defended you
as best I could,
until the very
very
end,

until you were ready to ascend.
God only knows the blend
of courage it took for you to extend
your empty hand to your impending
transcendence;
the best and strongest of all men,
even at the very end.
I'll now have to contend
with not being there to spend
your last moments with you
at the very
very
end.

What to do now?
Move on, but how?
Strong as an ox,
but not allowed your naval socks
in your wicker box,
in case of Covid aftershocks.
How can I forget our talks
and all our lovely rambly walks?
You might as well stop all the clocks,
cos time has slowed right down
to the equinox.

Empty funeral, keep your distance,
Father likens to a Mafia existence,
parties apart in their subsistence,
my mother cries without assistance,
baby sister brave in her consistence,

sit through 'Edelweiss' at his insistence.
We leave alone
without resistance.

Now you're really gone, it's true;
how to hold on? I hope you knew
by the memories you drew,
at the end.
Were they new?
Did they truly attend you?
I hope to God they befriended you,
and I hope you knew,
I hope you knew,
through
and through
and through,
just how much
I loved you.

For the family you were the glue,
and with your life we will now strew
our hopes
and dreams,
and all we pursue,
Grandpa, this I promise you.
Although we did not bid adieu,
nor say goodbye how I swore to you
we would,
as if I ever could
forget you,

I will not
forget you.

Of course I'll remember all our talks,
and all our lovely rambly walks;
I'll remember the smiles,
the twinkly eyes,
the quiet nodding from one so wise,
your tapping feet in your naval socks.
Don't worry,
I've got them,
they haven't been lost.
Carving the turkey, stoking the fire,
watching your paper rise higher and higher.

These are the memories that I will keep
where they'll be free to fly and leap,
and if, in the darkness, my mind starts to creep
to the sadness buried away down deep,
I'll remember that grief
is allowed to peep,
and it's healthy indeed
to allow it to sweep
over from time to time,
and to weep.
Because bereavement takes a lot of upkeep,
and the road to healing
can be
so
steep.

Beloved grandfather, high in the sky,
together with Granny, I know you'll be fine.
Although I will never quite understand why

this all got so crazy amplified,
I know it'll get easier to try
and move on
in the end
without ever having said goodbye.

I'll say goodbye as I frame your face,
and when I recall your strong embrace,
and when I truly remember the space
around you that was so quiet, I'll misplace
any worry
or panic
or fear.
No trace.

For the family you were the root,
and although it's difficult to compute,
all of your movements, however minute
have an impact on everything that I do.
Grandpa, this I promise you,
Grandpa, this I promise you:
although we did not bid each other adieu,

I will not
forget you.

I will not
forget you.

As if I ever could
forget you.

# HOW TO BREATHE

*David Bottomley*

Everything feels surreal
if you look at it long enough.
The rows of uniform terraced houses, neatly arranged,
even the repeat planting of trees                    in avenues,
everything seems regimented,                         unchanging,
like this life you find yourself surviving.

How on earth does each tree keep sane
when it's rooted to the same spot each day,
can never escape for a change of scenery?
How does it keep motivated,     focused,     alive,
weather the changing seasons,     shed inhibitions in fall,
bare its soul in winter and grow new shoots in spring,
increasing in size and stature,
each year another ring,     yet remain somehow
the same?

I've tried to be different kinds of tree,
but there's no mistaking my type of bark:
it's ingrained and rough to the touch;
my leaves will always be the same shape;
my canopy cannot camouflage my category.

I get ruffled by the same maddening winds
and burnt by the same summer sun,
but there are days when I'd rather be anyone;
Or maybe I just haven't learnt how to sink
my roots deep enough to draw on all the nutrients,
and goodness I need to grow and thrive
to become established in my own right.
I'm too busy
worrying if
my branches
are growing
in all the right
directions to
ever remember
how to breathe.

# I AM A GIRL OF MANY COLOURS

*Elisabeth-Rae Reynolds*

I am a girl of many colours –
I'm autistic, you see;
And though there are many others,
They're much different from me.

Though the same diagnosis,
There are no two the same;
This spectrum is endless;
Fighting stigma is my aim,

So before you make assumptions,
Let me get one thing straight:
Though my IQ may be high,
I often struggle to concentrate,

So…

Let's move on to what I'm good at!
Rhyming words is what I know –
I love the way the sounds all match,
Creating a satisfying flow,

But please don't change the placing
Of the clock upon my wall,

As coping with sudden changes
Is something I'm not good with at all;

My brain runs on routine,
Repetition, structure and a plan,
So I apologise for the inconvenience,
But I am doing the best I can.

I am a girl of many talents,
But I'm still learning social cues,
Forever trying to understand
People's ever-changing hues.

My senses always heightened,
Loud noises make me scream,
Though you won't hear me make a sound,
I'll bounce around to let off steam.

All I ask is for your patience –
Know I've be patient with you too;
Rip away the differences and you'll see
That I'm an awful lot like you.

I am a girl of many colours –
I'm autistic, you see;
And though there are many others,
They'll be like them, not like me.

## IF SOMEONE HAD ASKED ME WHY

*Ngoi Hui Chien*

I only stepped out of my house once
every fortnight when the first lockdown began in the UK
when the crowds receded from the roads
that crawled in a morbid gait towards the distance
I was locked in the room by fear
which could not be washed away
with soap that dwindled like my trove of food
so hunger coaxed my edgy guard to let me out
to the nearby store where my arm stretched its neck
hurriedly pecking at the cheap essentials
for the next fourteen days
of confinement, if someone had asked me why

The number of cases increased like the piles of items
on the counters waiting to be packed
in such a nonchalant society, ambushed
by the virus that pervaded the routine, like how
the land was flooded by yellow-skinned beings
such as me, someone holding a Malaysian passport
and my Chinese appearance was often the colour
of the nightmare, what right did I have to comment
on their outdoor activities ritualised
with much freedom, from the parks to the streets
when masks were claimed to be a mendacious camouflage

the fear sheltered underneath was fledging
so the sceptical eyes became more violent
and the fists got vociferous in a stir
of suspicion, an identity that spelt threats
and assaults, if someone had asked me

Why I scurried in between the shelves in the store
darting away from humans whose voices
scratched my eardrums like sirens of warning
progeny of horror that could seize the air behind my mask
the unspeakable drifting in the unnameable moment
upon isolation too long a time
the mornings had been flitting shadows of ghostly emotions
I rushed between my house and the store
as the finger was pointed at the Chinese who endured
with a frown on my face, if someone

Had asked me why, in my mind
laws sitting down one after another, would they not
be fined for not wearing masks, could they
still wander outside the houses, why
the news from the faraway continent would be transmitted
to this anguished soul who was locked here, in this place
I saw how the sheep with fleece fair and fluffy
drowned in the tranquil sea
so melancholically blue above my head
whenever I walked with haste to and from the store
with a mask that muffled the frightful scream
skulking below the rippling composure
for the next fourteen days

# LOCKDOWN ANTIDOTE:

## COLLE FIORITO – ROME

*Martin Bennett*

So all roads lead to Rome? A mere wish,
Given Draghi's now decreed the city
Out of bounds. Zoned orange-yellow, here
At the *periferie* we remain
*Lockati*; excuse the Itaglish –
Language also flexes a strange new strain.

Until stampeded by lawnmower's roar,
Tobina, from her corner-cushion,
Alternates catnaps with keeping watch
On gardens below – whisker, eye and claw:
How via bristling shrubbery, unkempt arbour,
Green conjures a spectrum of it own.

Toy windvanes recycle the rainbow;
Lopped tree heliports a whirrish dove.
Symmetries in fences, in hedgerows,
Ex-prof gets re-employed, would-be Pisarro,
Some neo- if anonymous Cezanne,
For easel, palette, brush just a biro.

À la Van Gogh, add a stand of iris;
Noon as mirror, upon opposite terrace
Fellow pensioner seeing out his days
This late April, under its still chill rays,
Closure another doldrum which passes?
More power to that peaked cap, a constant gaze.

# METAGENOMICS, CODING AND SPRING:

## THE MANY GREEN HUES OF FEARING THE UNKNOWN

*Ieva Dapkevicius*

### I. INTRODUCTION

In the morning, when I unlock it, the laboratory
Is empty and quiet, welcoming in its solitude,
Submerged in fuzzy heat and the smell of electronic devices,
Sun-warmed old plastic and paper binders.

Behind the dusty filter of the windowpane,
The trees sway their new buds,
Their green flags of not-giving-up-yet.

### II. MATERIALS & METHODS

I allow myself a moment to breathe.
Soon: centrifuge cycles, discarded pipette tips, the mental acrobatics
Of trying to make sense of the natural world without a supernatural mind.
For now, it is enough to put on my lab coat one arm at a time,
Picking out the unfortunate shards of glass from the pockets
One at a time, slipping on one blue latex glove at a time,
Snapping myself into place.

Time passes in a primed manner: forward, reverse.

### III. RESULTS

When I step outside again, head heavy with worry,
As DNA, stained SYBR green, zips and unzips, remakes itself
(Or so I hope – and don't we all long to be remade?)
As its strands run their electric crawl, their slow-mo race through Jell-O,
(Don't we all have nightmares just like that?)
I am hit by the bluntly green smell of cut grass.

### IV. DISCUSSION

I realise, with the hesitance of a non-epiphany,
That my work is small, not meaningless –
But the world goes on beyond my worrying.
Whether or not I decode its molecular gospel,
The grass goes on growing greener outside.

You watch it as I do, not noticing it,
Not thinking of lab work or DNA:
On your retinas, the cyber-green lines of code
Line up like stanzas of logic on mirror display,
And yet the grass goes on growing greener outside.

### V. CONCLUSION

I will let my days unfold as they will, my feet carry me where they must,
And I will remember an ink-green note scribbled on scrap paper:
I am content with this being just another experiment.

# OCCUPATION: HOUSEWIFE

*Sora Li Anders*

on the blank census of the 50s
with a husband and his shiny shoes
resting at the door
before he raises his fist
and dons them again.

i do not wish to hail from this era
as rain comes from thundering clouds
that spill their overflowing anger
onto the unsuspecting world below.
it is a dangerous place
of plastered smiles

and dead eyes
that belong buried in the backyard
with the family dog
that the four children did not
care for as they promised
the tattered woman with tired eyes.

yet i am sliced
from the moth-ball scented fabric
of this vanquished time
that refuses to accept its defeat
and lay in the man's grave,
in the warrior's grave.

the stitches in this painfully sewn coat
gifted from tired, lined hands,
coated in paraffin wax and lotion after nightfall,
however, are flagrantly illegal,
and will be until 1963,
when the mixing of silk and cotton thread

is finally allowed.
until then, i am trapped in the lingo
of an era that does not want me,
just as i reject it,
although we are both bound
by the careful mending

of the overworn apron-wearing shell
of the once-vibrant woman
who could have been the wind itself
if she had not been trapped
in a glass jar
for a man to observe and destroy.

i am the modernity that tradition despises,
as well as the tradition modernity strays from.
it is unfair; i belong nowhere,
and have no shelter to cower under
when the doors are broken by batons
and the screams of those

who cannot float with the canal's current,
but instead try to fight it
and return to the mouth of an ocean
that no longer exists,

replaced by metal doors
that do not open but by the command

of a man whose pockets droop
with the burden of turbid wealth
that he hides from the sweet-faced woman
who wrangles crying children
in his gilded home
as her tears polish the floor.

i never asked to be this weak,
a relic from a lost era that should not exist
with the intellect and drive
my foremothers fought to convince ignorant slobs
that we possess.
i am the greatest dream and nightmare

imaginable by the pallbearers of the past,
who sought to run into the thicket of thorns
and retreat into the waters
from which we sprung forth,
ready to breathe air and conquer
yet another domain.

my mascara runs down the polished cheeks
that make me desirable to those
who pretend they respect anything other
than the curve of my being,
who cast the illusion that they see my invisible mind,

doomed to create the genetic progeny
of a man who loves the curve of my eyes

and slope of my breasts,
as well as the swirling strokes of my mind
or words, but only in theory,
or when they come from the mouth of our son,

who will have my dark hair and smile
and elegance in the english language
(yes it has to be english), but unfettered
by the weakness of my femininity
or boundaries of my husband.
he will achieve great things that i should have,

but cannot. because
the scratched-out x that runs through
my vision and between my legs
defines me, although it should not.
no one should be like this any more –
this breed was supposed to die;

but i am still alive, against all odds.
the mayfly that will be dead in hours
but still refuses to succumb to human hands
and accept its early fate.
i cannot help but sit prettily within the confines
laid out by my father's fathers,

despite my best efforts
to wring my wrists raw with struggle
against the binds they shackled me with,
starting at birth
and unending at death,
and i am sorry.

# ON AMPUDIA'S *CRISANTEMI*

## IN THREE ACTS, BARCELONA 2020

*Jenna Pashley Smith*

One hundred thirty years earlier, the musician's elegy flowered
In the cool of night, notes unfurled on paper:
Black blooms, funereal blossoms for the memory of the dead.
Puccini composed an everlasting florescence,
A chrysanthemum he would pluck again and again,
For different strings, new arrangements.

The petals of this melody fall,
Drop gently on grieving ears,
A crescendo to lift wilted spirits.

Tonight, two thousand, two hundred and ninety-two palms,
Figs and other greenery sit poised on velvet seats,
Dressed in evening finery. Droplets of mist hang

Like diamonds from lobes and veins. In the boxes,
Heirs and royalty of the vegetable kingdom plant themselves
For a concert theirs and theirs alone.

Attuned to every vibration, stems bend low,
Spill over balconies, leaves crane to hear
Plaintive notes pulled from wood, from strings.

Rooted in place, these listeners respire
And purify air thick with sound. Entranced,
This unmasked audience sits expressionless

Under a cloudless dome. But who can be
Unmoved by the cello's rumble, the fluttering viola,
These gasping violins? Musicians bow, exit stage left.

No thunderous applause, no encore greets their retreat.
What thoughts rise and fall in the silence?
What verdant dreams grow in the darkness?

This is a time of chrysanthemums,
An intermission of mourning.
Houseplants hum a minor tune,

*Piano*, *pianissimo*,
Await gloved escorts to new homes.
Full to bursting with the luxuries of hope,

Its scent emanates through every pore
And membrane. No longer spectators,
They will intercede, embrace cloistered humanity,

Offer grace as air, a solitude shared,
Our entwined future curled tight as a song
In the ripening bud.

# ONE STRONG DAY

*J.L. James*

One tentative day
I will tip a toe
Away from you.

I will shed this stereotype,
Along with my armour
And my apprehension.

One confident day
I will know where I want to be
And how to get there.

I will leave you with dignity:
My tiptoes will become strides;
I will walk tall and straight.

One brazen day
I will sell your broken promises
And buy back my soul.

I will defibrillate my heart,
Gather up my spirit,
My pills and my brain.

One patient day
I will count to ten
And be calm in the face of you.

I will sleep soundly
Through the night
And delight in the dawn.

One decisive day
I will eat ice cream for breakfast
Just because I want to.

I will run loudly
Up and down the stairs
And slam all the doors.

One leisurely day
I will open my mail
Whenever I please.

I will annihilate my anxiety,
Fight my fears with ferocity
And free my future.

One determined day
My tears will dry;
I will hold my head high.

I will noisily chuck the cutlery
Back into the drawer
And clatter without calamity.

One courageous day
I will not fear questions
Or the sound of my voice.

I will not have to guess
The answer repeatedly
Until I get it right.

One serene day
I will answer to no one;
Ignore the phone and doorbell.

I will draw my curtains
And shut my door
In your face.

One bold day
I will speak
My mind.

The words formed in my brain
Will freely emerge
From my lips and be heard.

One daring day
I will ask for help
And receive it.

I will take a long soak
In the brimming bath
With the door closed.

One tenacious day
I will put on heavy boots
And my storm jacket.

I will stamp a steel-clad toe
All over your eggshells
And empty dreams.

One audacious day
I will smile and wave
And turn away from you.

I will put my brain in a bag
And my soul in a sack
To sling over my back.

One brave day
I will breathe
And believe in myself.

I will see.
I will feel.
I will rise.

One strong day
I will be me
Once more.

# PANDEMIC CLASSROOM

*Karin Molde*

This is my bag, this my folder.
It bears my name. This is
my red pen, this my memory stick.
When I lose it, I panic.

This is my chalk. Eat it, your voice
is velvet. This is my throat.
When I cough I am eyed.
This is my elbow. This is my mask.

My muffled voice like the victim's
tied to a chair, like the traitor's
on the intercom. These are

our books. These are my eyes.
Those are yours. You guide them
into mine, where they float like
waterlilies on a pond. These are

my crow's feet scratching
the soft skin of your stories.
You tell them, sing them,
like pond skaters do.

We lean in like bended torsos,
and the air is a bridge we can
walk on, and we listen.

These are our masks. They hang
in bushes at the side of the road.
They cling to grass, soaking up
last night's rain, used to
being drunk on our breath.

# PANDEMIC MUMS

*Kathryn Louise Knight*

Mum! Can we watch a film tonight?
Can we have nuggets for our tea?

Why don't you ask your dad? Or anyone who isn't me.

Can you watch the kids, babe? They are driving me bezerk!
I know I'm at the kitchen table, but I am still trying to work!

We should grab a coffee or walk around in two.
Can't you see I'm tired and socially distancing myself from you?

No travelling, no freedom, no chance to breathe or stop,
My only independence comes in the form of a weekly shop.

A mother, a colleague, a chef, a maid and wife –
But when do I get the chance to go back to normal life?

As much as I adore them, as much as I don't mind,
I'd love To venture out without my kids trailing behind.

I'd love to go back to the office and be around some peers;
Instead I'm in the bathroom fighting back my tears.

I've lost my independence and my identity away from home,
Constantly surrounded, but somehow all alone.

I'd like to think it's over soon, to be free and have some fun,
But then it's back to ironing, because a mum's work is never done.

A family, a home to keep and constant work-related calls
All become so tedious when you're stuck staring at the same four walls.

The only peace I seem to get is when everyone is in bed:
I relax in front of the telly with some chocolate and a glass of red.

I call my mum who lives away and we put the world to rights –
The only person who gets me through these otherwise boring nights.

The news is always gloomy, and the world is stuck in fear;
I don't think anyone could of anticipated this testing and trying year.

Covid jabs, mortality rates and crazy panic buys –
The masks don't seem to cover up the pain behind the eyes.

For everyone who's lost someone, whose worlds have been torn apart,
How do we got back to normal? How do we even start?

And when we feel like giving up and have taken all we can take,
We pick ourselves up, start again, for our loved ones' sake.

As sure as it all started, it certainly will end,
And then comes time for healing, not 'make do and mend'.

I lost my identity, but others have lost much more;
But every day I tell myself what I do this for:

I do this for my family, and they do this for me,
And despite my best efforts we're still having nuggets for our tea.

# PETROSINELLA[1]

*Rose Cook*

During lockdown I have fantasies about getting a puppy,
or kitten, guinea pig, rabbit, mouse... it appears I have regressed
to four again, longing for something furry to hold.

My granddaughter wears a full-length purple princess dress,
perhaps as a brilliant piece of subconscious, escapist theatre.
It is her Rapunzel dress, she tells me. But I am Rapunzel,
shut in my town house, shielding for the foreseeable future.
She laughs, thinks I am joking. Ha ha.
Granny in a long purple rustling dress and crown.
Where is your wand, then?

My wand is research. I eat parsley, which I love, find out that
the real Rapunzel was a third century saint called Barbara,
beheaded by her father. I see the similarities. She has her food
delivered in a basket on a rope and my house is tall with windows –
plus my dad did try to behead me, intellectually. Another version
has Rapunzel named after parsley, which she feeds to her rabbits.
My hair is growing long. I must break out.

---

1 *Petrosinella*: The old Italian word for parsley.

# POSTPARTUM

*Jessica Johnson*

Lockdown baby, here you are at last.
My baby, or is it our baby?
I carry and grow their hope, their silver lining,
Aware of the pressure, their reason to keep going.
Restrictions ease, the floodgates open,
Boundaries left at the door with no time to waste;
Everyone ramped up, everyone eager.
I laboured and birthed him, and now I hand him over.

Competing families staking their claims,
Taking family photos, but they don't mean me;
Analysing his features, but they've forgotten about mine;
The long awaited miracle, how truly divine.

I stand and I watch, my womb still aching.
How pleased I am he's loved so much.
Edging away, I leave them all to it;
My role is over, my body no longer needed.

But then a new lockdown, and we're all alone;
Groundhog Day, each one the same.
My new role is simple: keep everyone's miracle alive,
And don't forget to send photos for each day that goes by.

A never-ending cycle with no support in sight,
All sense of myself gone, my body is his:
He owns every minute, every hour, every day;
To submit to this reality, it's the only way.

I sometimes think the Stepford Wives had it right –
Switch off your needs,
Switch off your thoughts, your dreams, your mind.
I exist to serve; everything else I leave behind.

But one day soon I'll switch back on;
My life will return, my body will be mine.
These newborn days weren't made to last,
And I know in the future, I'll miss the past.

# PRIDE

*C.M. Rosier*

The Rainbow. Violet, indigo, blue…
Blue.. was that blue for my mood? Blue for the bruises?
Blue for the dress that the boy never chooses?
Let's try green.
Green for the grass on the other side –
Wait, which side were you on? How can it be both?
You only date guys.
Why not admit that you're telling us lies?
You're a fake,
You want attention;
People like you are not welcome at pride.

Yellow, like the bruises. No, I already mentioned those –
That's old news, Fake News, millennial woes.
Sorry, I've jumped to orange.

Yellow: isn't that a threat?
A warning?
Red skies at morning,
Storms dawning, skies turning black…
But that colour isn't in the rainbow, so let's move on.
In fact, let's backtrack.

Is pink in the rainbow? Pink is for girls, blue for boys, yellow is
for both…
No wait, not in that way.
I mean, it's just too difficult to call them 'they'.
They're getting confused, that's all it is.
Perhaps they spent too much time with *The Magic School Bus*
and Miss Frizz' –
They're getting ideas.

The type of thoughts that they teach us to fear:
They say ideas are dangerous, violent even. Red.
At what point was the sky supposed to fall when we wed?

And ideas grow like patina that's green.
The beauty that grows when we can finally breathe.
And they try so hard to scrub us back to perfection
They cannot see how good we look when we're wearing life.

And let me just say again, the sky did not fall when I chose a wife.
We were conscripted in this battle;
We did not choose this divide.
You are not the one whose mother cried
When he cut his long hair and asked for a pack of boxers.

Red is for lost mothers.
Indigo is for the nights wishing we could wake up as someone else.
Blue is for his eyes when he looked into the mirror with his
freshly cut hair
And finally saw himself
For the first time.
Yellow is for the morning when hope rises

And a hand reaches out to show you
That the sun shines on us all.
Orange is the light that washes over you
As you lie next to the one you love
And wake up to a new world.

Red skies at morning,
But a rainbow will follow the storm.

## SERTRALINE RESIN

*Anna Dallaire*

The parasite that did its best to kill me,
That needled its way through my guts
And crumpled me like a piece of paper,
Is trapped in resin,
And it looks small.

I hold it up and stare at it;
It stares back at me.
The tables have turned,
For it is no longer me who is paralysed
    in a see-through prison,
Seeing the world and knowing
    it can do nothing to free me.

I will take a morbid delight
In hanging this on my wall,
Point to it for guests and say,
'Look at the poison that was in me'.

## SICK RAPUNZEL

*Charlotte Murray*

My first night out in three years. She doesn't ask why.
Just turns up at my door in a tiny pale-blue dress
the colour of summer skies I've missed.
I wear black, of course, though I can no longer
remember which part of me I'm grieving for.

I take baby-bird steps, even in flats.
She towers above me like the bedroom walls
I've grown accustomed to. Her hair is spun silk
that she threads through my fingers
as though she wants me to climb up. I don't tell her

that sometimes at night I'm driving and see her
in the distance, grinning with her thumbs hooked
over the pockets of her leather jacket
like in her profile picture, but then the earth stops
and I hit water and wake, choking.

Bluebells ring out down the lane. A scent
I've only known before in the cold half-conscious dawn
when steady rain turns ivy to satin,
when sheets cling wet as leaves. There is no witch
holding me captive. The witch is in me.

We don't make it to the pub.
Just lie there among wild grasses,
my shorn fuzz sticking up like weeds.
She lets me rest my head on her shoulder
as if it's the whole world, heavy and plundered.

# STONES

*Christian Ward*

*Queer*, the first stone that was hurled,
Almost hit the back of my head.
I picked it up and let it sink
To the bottom of a jacket pocket.
Its warm autumnal colours glowed
At night. Attracted foxes, blackbirds
And butterflies. Wildflowers poked
Their heads from the wardrobe.
*Poor*, the second stone that was hurled,
Reeked of the sea. Transparent as glass,
I saw a diorama inside its delicate shell:
A crumbling seaside town. Conger eels
Wrapping themselves around the pier's
Welted legs. The dying light of a shutting-
Down fairground. I carefully wrapped it
In newspaper and placed it in a shoebox
Next to the heater in my bedroom.
*Disabled*, the last stone that was hurled,
Was wrinkled like an oak in a drought.
Its surface almost burned to the touch.
Hard to see if anything was inside.
I buried it in a pot filled with soil outside
And prayed for rain. I never saw the faces

Of those who hurled these stones,
Never understood their need to silence me.
I stored each one carefully, handling
Them like children. 2021 will be the year,
I tell myself, when they will transform,
When I will need to let go.

# THE COUNTRY CALLED NEW BEGINNING

*Priyanka Kelly Burns*

In our camp we sat waiting.
Ma had said that we would leave for our new beginning tomorrow night, and I remember asking her, 'Ma, where is New Beginning? Is it far away?'
She'd smiled a real smile and told me we were so close.
I remember how we slept outside at night.
The frost on my back helped by the heat of my chest. We slept facing each other, my ma hugging me so tightly into herself. Her slender, strong arms were my cage against the cold night.
I would wake with dew on my brown-white vest;
I knew it wasn't sweat, as I was too young for that.

When it got very dark a man came and told Ma something that made her cry.
She picked me up and carried me to where the others were.
I could hear the lapping waters just down the hills of sand.

Ma had told me that was a beach when we arrived at the new camp.
She said we would play in the water another day, but not now.

I know now that it was the sea that I saw on the first day. The barren but boundless blue which moved like the wind in the tall grasses from where I was from.

We began to advance, shoeless soldiers in a line.
I couldn't see it, but I heard the boat.
We all got on; my ma was still carrying me tightly to herself, my arms and legs wrapped around her.

As we moved from shore to shoals and gained great speed, an old man from the camp fell off the back of the boat, but they kept going, even though Ma and the ladies screamed.
We didn't stop for him, and I cried.
That was the worst part. And then I think I fell asleep.

'Ma,' I had awoken with questions when I could see the sky was light blue and felt that we were just swaying.
'Ma?'
'Hm?' She touched the top of my head with her trembling, tender lips.
'Did we reach New Beginning?'
She looked down at my face; she had begun to cry.
She kissed me again, on each eyelid, her tears falling on my cheeks.
'Yes,' she said.

# THE DAY YOU STOP SURVIVING

*Sophie Sparham*

AFTER CAROLINE BIRD

You lift your head from the toilet bowl and think, I didn't die tonight. And the doctors come and the dosage gets bigger and the pantomime continues and they always cast you as the back end of the donkey, even though the show is titled in your name. Have you tried living? your therapist asks, as though it's a holiday destination you haven't visited, and you wonder how you can live when there are dishes in the sink and bills on the floor and a pile of logs in the garden you've been ignoring since March. I'll consider it, you respond. You go home and buy a smoothie machine, blend strawberries and bananas, sit on the bench outside and drink. Maybe this is what she meant, you think. So, you purchase more fruit until the excess rots your pantry and you're forced to start a compost bin. You adopt a dog and a plant and take them both on walks down the Derwent canal. Oh, this is definitely living, you think. Until the dog eats the plant and you question its morals. You learn how to drive a speedboat, then a plane; practice your Bond villain laugh. Is this living? You bake a cake out of old bike parts and present it to the local Rotary club. Is this living? You learn to bowl barefoot and crack a raw egg on your head before every game. Is this living? You join a Led Zeppelin cover band, where everyone calls you Stan and as you sit and smoke in the back of the van; you wonder, Is this living? Am I doing it? You jump out of a plane from seventeen thousand feet, and as you fall, you think, Am I living now? Is this living? You shed the skin of industry and become a caretaker at a French monastery. Surely, this has got to be living. But the floors are never clean, and the people talk about enlightenment as if it is something they purchased off Amazon. You go to the doctors and tell them you think you are dead. The doctor asks if you've been taking your new medication and why your dog has a perm like Brian May. You go home and wash the dishes, pay the bills, pull the axe from the garden shed and begin to chop. The sun catches the back of your neck; maybe this year you will get a tan.

# THE GIFT

*Voirrey Faragher*

We have been gifted a silence of late,
have breathed in the morning air,
and in the evenings, which are filled with stars,
have taken it with us into our house
and allowed it to inhabit us.

The bamboo is taller by the back door:
new shoots grow by stealth, heaving skywards.
Our cat stretches out on the path, assured that we
are near, glad of each day that we offer our protection,
and in the pond the newts wriggle their little legs
and dive beneath the lily pads, and within the silence,
the bees buzz incessantly in the comfrey and in the poppies.

Each evening we notice the sky: a turquoise,
then turning dark and bats flying.
Every night a glory, a stillness which is holy.
We sit, touch each other, speak without words.

The tree will speak through their scars
of floods, heat, the plague which feasted upon us.
There is talk of renewal and rebirth, new ways
of doing things, a new beginning and a better end.
We sit and touch each other, speak without words.

# THE RACE

*Oyinmiebi Youdeowei*

R is for rioters: they loot and vandalise,
But can you for a second see the fear in their eyes,
The fear that they're next, the next to die?
Yet you call them criminals, instead of asking why.

A is for athletic: the many trophies won;
But this is a race, a race that can't be outrun.
Ever wondered why we sprint – is it to escape reality?
It's because we're accustomed to chains. Still, we try to
 break free.

C is for culture – what's left of it at least:
We tell tales of our heroes, while we are painted as beasts.
When our stories are told, they are washed to be fair,
Like the man who had a dream, instead of the one
 living a nightmare.

E is for ever – at least, until we decide:
Decide that we will all fight for what's right, to seal the
 divide,
To be equal, in our status, rights and opportunity,
Because I have hope, hope that one day we will finally
 be free.

# THE SONG

*Molly J. Evans*

From the rubble of dusk
Was born a song, chaos ordered
Into melody; shaded trees whimpered
In agitation, for they could not hear;
Neither could the glow of stars,
The moon or sea, in its tidal
Drum effort, up and down, back and
Forth; still, the feeling was never
Quite grasped. You see, the song, it crawled
Out from cavernous heart,
Molten like lava, cementing
Itself a home in each mind.
Man spluttered and choked,
Gasping to give it life, make it real,
For aeons tracing
Dawn like a vagabond sailor, needing
To claim that ecstatic pulse
In our very own hands.
So we harnessed the sun,
And thus the song became our blood
And bones, like sweet ichor,
Flowing golden, golden for ever.
But we were never truly God;

And though the song gave warmth
It twisted every sinew
Into fire, untameable, a chorus left empty.
We resolved to force our love
Into books, poems, art; a solemn eternity,
Yearning for truth.
They've muted the song now,
Labelled it seditious.
It'll be quiet for a while. But
From the rubble the song will rise
As always: a phoenix bursting into glorious flames.
On that day, people will gather
In the streets and tremor with joy,
The prospect of freedom and love and victory.
That day will come, that day will come.
Until then, you must keep on quietly humming.

# THE UPHOLDING

*David Hensley*

We were held, but we could not hold
Each other from our separate house arrests,
Could not meet in our customary groups
In our customary rooms, speak
Our minds in shouts or whispers, hear
The unspoken frown or smile, touch
Hands or cheeks for comfort.
Now we are slowly being released,
Baby rabbits emerging blind, stumbling
Over new routes, up old steps, seeking
Gallery openings and rescheduled symphonies, reaching
Out to hold our families and favourites.

If I hold up my hand will you see me?
If I reopen my heart will you come in?

## TO A FRIEND

*Ella Dane-Liebesny*

I have known you in the winter,
wholeheartedly. We left messages unspoken in crumb-laden
    pockets:
could we read them like tea leaves?
Do not be afraid to love.
Do not be afraid of being half-loved,
almost, temporarily.
One day I will be nothing but a breath in your lungs.
A poem you wrote when you were young.
(I hope not.)

Already we have forgotten how to run, relentlessly, in the
    direction of our dreams.
We remind each other, gentle in the stillness of dawn,
    unruptured fog. We do not touch but I hold you with me.

Everything comes from dust, but we came from crisp leaves.
We stumbled from trees (ancient) into each other's arms, the
    both of us ready to
catch. A gesture toward home –
yearning for sanctuary, seeking comfort and finding it.
We throw the bones again with ease,
ivory unsaid and unsayable.

Silently, somewhere, a star sheds its skin.

A silvery pause; something bound to part us, but,
all of a sudden,
bound together.

# TRAPPED

*William Foster*

Dazed and confused in a troubled mind, yet still here, inside but unable to find. Trapped and deceived with no way out, with a silent voice I scream and shout. But no one can hear my silent groan; I'm on a different wavelength, a different tone. I find it difficult to think or communicate, to say what I mean or have a debate. As life goes on all around me; I have no input. I'm trapped, you see. It's unfair – I've had enough; my memories are fading of people and stuff. Sometimes there is a flash of light, one that shines so very bright. A memory flickers from the past, but disappears again, oh, so fast. Restless and anxious and wanting to shout, I take more time to work it out. Frustrated and angry with tears I hate, I find it so difficult to speak or communicate. Strangers appear and say, There, my friend. When will my nightmare ever end? I miss our chats over cakes and tea. Life's not fair – this shouldn't happen to me. When I speak the words don't make sense; they come out all jumbled and make me tense. My brain is dying cell by cell; dementia really is a living hell.

# TREADING CAREFULLY

*Nisha Bhakoo*

Yes, I know I have eaten too much chocolate today.
I refuse to feel shame for seeking comfort.
Granules of hot chocolate bittering the tongue.
Wonders in the cupboard. Treading carefully.
You see me sneaking the last bar.
The underworld has lost all of its horror
Now that I live with you.
I try to process – new shadows, the German news.

Like love letters in an envelope,
I slip each sharp piece between my lips.
Marzipan centre. I have nothing to confess
But the world.

Scorching the top of my mouth.
A boil, a mutter under your breath.
I know I scare you a lot,
Locking myself into the bathroom.

Hammering sigils into our floorboards.
Painting my nails with the occult.
I crave a new chapter.
But I swallow my voice.

We were swept up in the perfume of lust
When we rushed into a life together.
Now I use too much toothpaste,
Hold the pendulum on every decision,

Eat all of our chocolate.
But you eat all the bread!
I live brightly most days, frequently, not always.
I love you most days, often, fully, still.

# TSUNAMI

*Aly Lou Smith*

My husband dreamt we were in a tsunami;
We were trapped inside a house in an air bubble,
Holding each other tight as the water surrounded the building.
Were we scared? I asked him,
Hoping it was an adventure dream where we would swim to the surface,
Saving women and children in addition to ourselves.
'Yes, we were scared,' he said.
'We were absolutely bloody terrified.'
April was a tough month. Financially frightening;
Our future still looks uncertain.
Physical and emotional illnesses erupted to the surface,
And several rejections from art funds and government support schemes
Causing blind panic – on occasion so overwhelming that we would be lying
If we told you we had not considered,
On more than one occasion,
Leaving it all behind.
And not in a good way.

But we think of the sadness that this would cause,
And what would happen if one survived: it would break the other

Over and over and over again with grief, remorse and guilt.
Explaining to friends and family why we didn't ask for help
And took that most drastic, mainly untalked-about, path.
So together we will keep going, dreaming of the rainbows
that must appear after the tsunami.
Planning the visits, the contacts, the arms that will envelop us;
That and other little things to keep us from drowning.

## WALK AWAY

*Peter Hill*

Turn around and don't look back –
There's nothing more to say.
When it's over and all is said and done,
It's best to walk away.

When all that was is now no more
And nothing good remains,
There's no point in clinging to the past;
Accept it's time for change.

But change is never easy –
It always comes at a cost.
When faced with its reality,
We only see the loss.

This sense of loss we feel;
With it brings doubts and other fears.
By instigating changes,
Will this bring yet more bitter tears?

But to stay where we are,
To just accept the status quo,
Only serves to underline
That there's now nowhere else to go.

So instead of looking back,
Focus on where you need to be;
Let go of all that holds you back,
And from the past be free.

# WHEN I COME OUT

*Hannah Ross*

When I come Out,
The house will burn
With a deep, dark
'You'.
The 'I' and 'we'
Will
Curl and cripple
Until they rest as the
Ashes
Upon my face.
When I come out,
Your tongue will lash
And wrap my ears with wet claims.
You will split me at the seams:

'This is evil.'

And apples and palms will be thrown in righteousness
As you speak.

When I come out,
Out into that which is simultaneously
Nothing new and everything unholy,
You hit me with a
Silence.

That
Silence
Is bigger than me,
Bigger than you,
And sinfully –
Though you would deny it –
Bigger than Him.

And so, when I come out,
I will walk from this Eden of erasure,
Beyond and to an outside.
An outside that is mine,
Not yours,
Not His.

And maybe one day,
After this rapture happens,
He will forgive you.

I'm not sure if I ever will.

## WOMAN

*Jasmine Kaur*

i know that i am woman
i feel it inside my chest
and it has nothing to do with breasts

but i don't know what makes me woman
other than this wanting to be
and to keep being
woman

how can i say what it means to be woman
when i deny all definitions?
and w h y
should i know what is a woman?
does a man know what is a man?
he doesn't think
that it means
to be man
because the world bends for him

i know that men bend too
but masculinity hasn't been stained like femininity
masculinity did not have to fight for respect
masculinity has been seen as human
femininity as alien

to be woman
is to feel woman
every second
every minute

to forget your gender is a privilege
or madness

i feel woman
because we talk in a language designed for men
'what's up, guys?' 'hey, bro' 'duuude'
i feel woman when i can't help but hear
the silences of women
in the stories of men
because we have been told to shut up
to not draw attention
become invisible

i feel woman

in this poem
i feel woman
because i am

# ABOUT THE POETS

SORA LI ANDERS *p. 51*

Sora Li Anders was born and raised in Guam, a US territory in the Pacific Ocean. Since writing her first couplet declaring an undying love for pizza at age five, she has been a prolific author of varyingly disturbing prose. The recent and unexpected discovery of the notes app on her phone has further facilitated her creative ventures. She is currently a high school student residing in California.

LUCY BECKLEY *p. 23*

Lucy Beckley is a writer, wanderer and wonderer. She can often be found trailing after her children on the beach, taking a moment to catch her breath, soak up the sunshine and find the beauty and joy in the unseen and seemingly ordinary. She's worked in a range of roles in Marketing and Communications in the UK, Germany and Portugal and has a Master's in European Cultures. She also worked for a couple of years as a flower grower and florist in Cornwall. Her writing and poetry has appeared in a range of independent magazines and books. She is currently working on a novel and her first collection of poetry.

HEINRICH BEINDORF *p. 19*

Born and raised in a German coal-mining town, Heinrich studied modern languages and literature in Munich, Toronto and the USSR. After some *sturm and drang* years involving faraway continents, old vans and stark creative penury, he settled in Cologne, where he has been living and working as an author, translator and court interpreter since 1985. His poems, short stories and crime fiction have appeared in newspapers, poetry mags and anthologies, as well as on radio and the web. Seeing language reduced to verbiage for the purposes of dystopian political, economic and technological gospels makes his veteran wordmonger's heart ache.

MARTIN BENNETT *p. 47*

Martin Bennett lives in Rome where he teaches and contributes occasional articles to *Wanted in Rome*. He was the 2015 winner of the John Dryden Translation prize.

NISHA BHAKOO *p. 97*

Nisha Bhakoo has three poetry collections published: *You Found a Beating Heart* (The Onslaught Press, 2016), *Black & White Dream* (Broken Sleep Books, 2018) and *Spectral Forest* (The Onslaught Press, 2020). She edited *Contemporary Gothic Verse* for The Emma Press in 2019.

DAVID BOTTOMLEY *p. 40*

David Bottomley is a poet, playwright and librettist originally from Whitby. He was shortlisted for the Nick Darke Award for his play, *Waterton's Wild Menagerie*. He performed in his one-man show, *Message in a Bottle*, at the Edinburgh Fringe Festival. His play, *The Peacock and the Nightingale* was produced at the San Diego International Fringe Festival, and *Britain for Breakfast* was a finalist at the Enter Stage Write Awards at Birmingham Hippodrome in 2020. He was recently awarded second prize in the E.H.P. Barnard Poetry Prize 2021. During lockdown he collaborated with fifty creatives to interpret fifty poems on film for his *Poetry Film Festival*.

ALLIE BULLIVANT *p. 31*

Allie Bullivant is a writer whose work could be (but so far hasn't been) described as the ginger lovechild of Mary Oliver and the Coen Brothers. Her writing has been featured in *The Critic*, *The Cardiff Review*, *Dappled Things* and *Oxford Culture Review*. She is a Long Island native but currently resides in Virginia with her husband and daughter.

PRIYANKA KELLY BURNS *p. 81*

Priyanka Kelly Burns is a storyteller at heart. Kelly (as she is affectionately known), is in Law School in the South West of England, where she currently resides. She is proudly South African: born in Durban, KwaZulu-Natal and raised in Cape Town. Kelly is a writer of poetry, short stories and fiction. This is her first published piece of writing but certainly won't be the last. Kelly is a comedian (according to her mom), an Aquarius (according to her birth certificate) and an adrenaline junkie to the nth degree. Her passions include, but are not limited to: meditation; swimming (in the sea or with sharks, or both); kick-boxing; reading; debating; gaming; volunteering; and, of course, writing.

LAURA CHOUETTE *p. 13*

Laura Chouette published her first poetry collection *When Dusk Falls* in 2020. She was born in Austria and discovered her passion for writing in early childhood years. Later, she found her love for the English language after seeing Oscar Wilde's play *The Canterville Ghost* at the age of twelve. In 2018, she completed her First Certificate in English (Cambridge English) and later attended classes in English Literature at the Paris-Lodron-Universität in Salzburg to improve her language skills and writing style. She is currently studying law and economy while working in her free time on a new poetry collection.

ROSE COOK *p. 67*

Rose Cook is a poet based in the South West. She co-founded the popular Devon poetry and performance forum One Night Stanza, as well as a poetry performance group Dangerous Cardigans. She has worked as an Apples and Snakes poet for over a decade, performing in many venues. Her poetry has been published in six collections; her latest book is called *Shedding Feathers* (published by Hen Run, Grey Hen Press).

ANNA DALLAIRE *p. 75*

Anna Dallaire was born in Montreal, Canada, and moved to the UK in 2007. She loves reading and the power of words. She is now a student at Plymouth University in her final year of a Bachelor degree in Illustration. She hopes to continue illustrating her own poetry after she graduates.

ELLA DANE-LIEBESNY *p. 93*

Ella Dane-Liebesny is a student from London. She is currently finishing her Bachelor degree in Sociology and Social Anthropology at the University of Cambridge, where she is President of Girton Poetry Group. She's been writing poetry for most of her life, and hopes to have a book of it one day. When not writing poetry, she can be found at Girton FemSoc, baking for her flatmates, or studying one of the many languages she hopes to learn.

IEVA DAPKEVICIUS *p. 49*

Ieva Dapkevicius is a poet and biochemist from the Azores, Portugal, born into a Lithuanian-Portuguese family in 1998.

Her first book was published at the age of nine (*The Golden Horse*, a children's fairy tale), and she has never stopped writing since, in parallel with her scientific pursuits. She has retained her fascination with fantasy and the natural world, two anchors in her creative work, as she navigates homesickness, loneliness and the anxieties inherent to one's early years. She is the founder of the Orangery Literary Society, a small but vibrant online community for up-and-coming poets and writers worldwide.

### CATHERINE EDMUNDS *p. 17*

Catherine Edmunds is a writer, portrait artist and professional violinist. Her published works include two poetry collections, five novels and a Holocaust memoir, as well as numerous short stories and poems in journals including *Aesthetica*, *Crannóg* and *Ambit*. She has been nominated three times for a Pushcart Prize, shortlisted in the Bridport Prize four times, and was the 2020 winner of the Robert Graves Poetry Prize. Catherine is married and lives in historic Bishop Auckland, in the foothills of the Pennines in the North of England.

### MOLLY J. EVANS *p. 89*

Molly J. Evans is an 18-year-old poet from South Wales. She is soon to be a student of English Language and Literature at Balliol College, Oxford. She is a keen photographer, writer and musician, and is working towards a career in novel-writing, politics or journalism.

### VOIRREY FARAGHER *p. 85*

Voirrey is an active feminist, socialist and Quaker. She lives in Cornwall with her husband, close to their three sons, who live in Cornwall and Devon. It is wild, there, in so many ways – close to the sea, the valleys and the moorland. Voirrey was unemployed in her younger years, and later worked with people whose mental health had been injured by their life experiences. Later she became a commissioner of services. She belongs to the North Cornwall Poetry Stanza, and loves it, as well as her fellow poets. They sustain each other.

WILLIAM FOSTER *p. 95*

Born in Govan, Glasgow, William moved south to look for work in 1974, and found himself working in a factory, where he remained for forty-five years. Since retiring in 2019, he spends his days gardening and walking the dog; this relaxed and peaceful existence gave him the time to redress priorities, and he found himself writing poems whilst walking the dog. Although the poems started out just as a bit of fun, and largely relating to family, they've taken on a life of their own.

JOHN GALLAS *p. 33*

John Gallas is an Aotearoa Poet, presently living in Leicestershire. He is published mostly by Carcanet, as well as by Five Leaves, Indigo Dreams, Cold Hub (NZ), New Walk Editions, SLG Press, Cerasus Publishing and Agraphia Press. He is the poet for St Magnus Festival, Orkney, and the Saxonship Project. He runs a month-by-month poetry website, and his latest book, *The Extasie* (Carcanet) was a *Sunday Times* Summer Reading choice. He is a fellow of the English Association, a biker and a tramper.

ROSIE GLIDDON *p. 5*

Rosie Gliddon was born and raised in Chelmsford, Essex, and now lives in London, where she has resided for the last few years. After studying English Literature at College in Southend-on-Sea, Rosie went straight into employment and is a corporate banker in London. Her passion, however, remains writing poetry, and she regularly develops her ideas on her daily commute into the City. When not writing, you can find Rosie cooking, reading, watching football and spending time with her family and friends. It is Rosie's dream to one day write a novel and have it published.

MARTHA GROGAN *p. 3*

Martha Grogan is a writer from the Isle of Wight. They're in their final year at the University of Kent, studying literature, creative writing and journalism. They live in Canterbury with their housemates.

DAVID HENSLEY *p. 91*

David Hensley is a poet, writer and brand consultant. Originally from Liverpool, he has lived and worked in Europe, Africa, Asia and the Middle East, but is now more prosaically based in Tunbridge Wells. He is the Chair of the Kent & Sussex Poetry Society (founded in 1946 by Vita Sackville-West) and former Chair of Creative Conscience, a charity whose mission is to embed purpose-driven creative thinking into organisations around the world, encouraging the creative community to use their talents for positive social and environmental impact.

ELLIE HERDA-GRIMWOOD *p. 35*

Ellie Herda-Grimwood studied English Literature and Music at university, followed by a Master's degree in Film Music and Opera. She attended a one-off poetry class in early 2021 (put on by her workplace) whilst also doing a course of bereavement counselling. The two experiences pleasantly collided, leaving a lasting impact and merging to inspire her first poem 'God Only Knows the Blend'. She is eternally on a relentless hunt for inner peace and – when not staring wistfully out of windows – can usually be found at the theatre, reading, playing piano, building Lego, watching Judy Garland films or eating pizza. She lives in London with her lovely supportive wife.

PETER HILL *p. 101*

Born in the village of Haydock, formerly in West Lancashire, Peter is the second eldest of four children born to working-class parents Leslie and Shirley Hill. His earliest influence came from an uncle who was a published poet and gifted artist in oils. After an eight-year hiatus, Peter began writing poetry again during the early part of 2021. Inspiration for poems is drawn from people, life, events and all things related to being human and the human condition.

SIMON JACKSON *p. 21*

Simon Jackson has had more than twenty plays performed, and was British Gas Young Playwright of the Year when he was still a young playwright. His poetry is published internationally, and he has won several awards. His short films with Scottish poets Billy Bragg and Franz Nicolay have been screened by the BBC, *Rolling Stone* and at film festivals around the world, and his play, *Turning to the Camera* was the *Guardian*'s Pick of the Week for Scottish theatre. He's never come close to making a living through the arts; he teaches Film in Shanghai, where he lives with his wife and two children and plays sax in the jazz-punk band Hogchoker.

### J.L. JAMES *p. 57*

J.L. James studied Creative Arts at university before later training to become a nurse. During the pandemic she rekindled her passion for creative writing and began entering poetry competitions. Since learning to read as a young child she has read daily throughout her life, and finds solace in the power of words. She has dreamed for many years of her writing making it into print and 'One Strong Day' is her first published work.

### JESSICA JOHNSON *p. 69*

Originally from Darlington, Jessica studied Law at Newcastle University, focusing on public international law and human rights. After graduating, Jessica moved to London to work in the charity sector, particularly on projects concerning homelessness and housing. Writing has always been a passion of hers, which she has worked on alongside her charity roles. The lockdowns of 2020 allowed her to focus solely on this, with 'Postpartum' being her first published poem. Jessica now lives in Walthamstow, East London, with her partner, Matt, and their one-year-old son, Nico.

### JASMINE KAUR *p. 105*

Jasmine Kaur is a queer writer/artist born in Moga, Punjab, and raised in too many places to name here. She likes to surround herself with stories and poetics in any medium, including audio, video, still images and performance. She decided to be a part-time poet as a twelve-year-old, and has continued to find joy in writing poetry since. She's currently a Master's in Philosophy student at Delhi University.

KATHRYN LOUISE KNIGHT *p. 63*

Kathryn was born and raised in east London by her loving working-class family. Despite struggling at school, she enjoys writing short stories and poems, and believes everyone should be able to express themselves, regardless of their education or upbringing. Kathryn is an avid reader and enjoys Stephen King's works. She has moved to Leeds to be with her partner and start her family, and hopes to continue writing while she juggles her work and family life.

LIZZY LISTER *p. 15*

In order to support her career as a poet, Lizzy Lister plays live soundtracks to silent films with the band Wurlitza and rents out Victorian railway carriages to holiday-makers in the Cornish village of St Germans. When not playing music, gardening, eco-warrioring, writing, cycling or painting, she can be found on the dance floor, or frolicking in the sea.

KARIN MOLDE *p. 61*

Karin Molde feels at home in Germany, Ireland and Tanzania. She is a teacher of German and English, and has been published in magazines like *The Honest Ulsterman*, *Light Journal for Photography and Poetry*, *The Blue Nib*, and in anthologies including *Everything That Can Happen. Poems About the Future* (Emma Press, 2019), *Identity* (Fly on the Wall, 2020) and *Remembering Toni Morrison* (Moonstone Press, 2020). Her poems written in Low German have been published in *Quickborn*, a magazine of modern literature in the West Germanic language. She is a member of the online poetry group Poets Abroad.

CHARLOTTE MURRAY *p. 77*

Charlotte is an archivist and writer from West Yorkshire. She won second place in *Bangor Literary Journal*'s Forty Words Competition 2021 and in *Lucent Dreaming*'s Poetry Competition 2021, was shortlisted in the Hive Young Writers' Competition 2020 and the Lord Whisky Sanctuary Poetry Competition 2020, and was longlisted for the Dead Cat Poetry Prize 2021. She has been published in *Bangor Literary Journal*, *CP Quarterly*, *Lucent Dreaming*, the *Mancunian Ways* anthology (Fly on the Wall Press) and is due to be published in *the winnow*.

NGOI HUI CHIEN *p. 45*

Ngoi Hui Chien is a Malaysian who will soon pursue a PhD in English literature at Victoria University of Wellington. He also holds an MA in the same subject from the University of Leeds. His research interests encompass, but are not limited to, trauma literature, postcolonialism, psychoanalysis, philosophy and ecocriticism. Other than literary criticism, he is committed to creative writing, too – especially poetry. He is highly passionate about anglophone and sinophone literatures, which are the two spheres of cultures that inspire his work. His English poems have been, or are due to be, published in the *Journal of Postcolonial Writing*, *New Writing: The International Journal for the Practice and Theory of Creative Writing*, *SARE: Southeast Asian Review of English* and *Transnational Literature*.

JENNA PASHLEY SMITH *p. 55*

Jenna Pashley Smith is a writer and poet from the Midwestern United States. Her essays, short stories, and poems have appeared in *Kaleidoscope*, *The Annals of Internal Medicine*, *East-*

*ern Iowa Review*, *The Binnacle* and others. She is currently at work on a young-adult novel in verse. When not immersed in a book or a poem, Jenna raises chickens and children in the suburbs of Houston, Texas, and dabbles in myriad artistic endeavours.

ELISABETH-RAE REYNOLDS *p. 43*

Elisabeth-Rae Reynolds is a proud activist for human rights and an aspiring actor and writer from London. After studying both Science and Art & Design at New City College, she then went on to study Human Biology at Canterbury Christ Church University. Whilst studying she was nominated for and awarded the Jack Petchey Award for Outstanding Achiever. Currently living in London, she now plans to follow her passions by delving into the arts and advocating for injustice and inequality.

HEATHER RODGERS *p. 11*

Heather Rodgers is an Ancient and Mediaeval History student at the University of Birmingham, and has previously been a runner-up in the 2018 Worcestershire Young Poet Laureate competition. She is keen to write more poetry and fiction across different genres, with a particular interest in personal narratives.

C.M. ROSIER *p. 71*

Originally from Malvern, C.M. Rosier studied Ancient History and Archaeology at the University of Birmingham before moving on to become a book promoter for many wonderful publishers. Now living in Staffordshire, Rosier focuses on their own writing, exploring their love of history through a modern lens.

HANNAH ROSS *p. 103*

Hannah grew up in Southampton, and then went on to study Religion and Theology in Bristol. She spends much of her time writing sapphic fantasy stories, though poetry was her first love. She was previously been commended for her poetry, which was entered into a competition hosted by the Young Poets Network. Hannah is currently studying her MA while frantically trying to piece together her first novel, which she may or may not finish. Her entry into the *New Beginnings* poetry anthology will be the first time her writing has been published.

KAY SAUNDERS *p. 27*

Kay Saunders is a seventeen-year-old from the Cotswolds who has been writing creatively her whole life. A core source of her inspiration has come from her experiences as someone within the LGBT+ community, which powers her to create heartfelt narratives that are relatable and a safe place for people to feel seen and understood. Between short stories, flash fiction and poetry, Kay has won local awards for her writing and recognition from publishers and authors, and hopes to soon join her literary idols in a world of publication.

MELISSA SIA *p. 7*

Melissa is originally from Liverpool and now lives in Glasgow. They draw inspiration from existing authentically as themselves and using this to embrace those who feel they cannot be visible just now. Poetry inspires them to create something physical from non-physical pain, a way of taking ownership and pride in their experiences, as well as that of their community. They completed a Master's degree in Gender Studies, and their final piece focused on lifting the voices of minority groups and exploring the fundamental healing nature that poetry has on those living with trauma. Outside of their busy working life, they revel in the calmness of their free time and believe there is beauty in the gentle rumbling of change.

ALY LOU SMITH *p. 99*

Aly Lou Smith works as a visual artist based in Newcastle upon Tyne. She writes on the side, mainly about her lived experience of Bipolar. Throughout 2021 her practice has evolved to be dominated by poetry, which gave her a therapeutic outlet and a way to record middle-aged, married life. Aly often considers herself unable to fit into 'normal' society due to her mental health diagnosis; however, her poetry has shown her just how reassuringly mundane her life actually is.

SOPHIE SPARHAM *p. 83*

Sophie Sparham is a poet and writer from Derby. She has written commissions for BBC Radio 4, The V&A and The People's History Museum. She co-hosts Word Wise, which won best spoken-word night at the 2019 Saboteur Awards. Her latest collection *The Man Who Ate 50,000 Weetabix* came out in April via Verve Poetry Press. Sophie's work has been published in *Orbis*, *Under the Radar* and *The Morning Star*. Her poem 'Sunrise Over Aldi' won third place in the 2020 Charles Causley International Poetry Competition.

LYNNE TAYLOR *p. 25*

Lynne lives in Didsbury, Manchester. Her poems have been published in anthologies and magazines including *PN Review*,

*Stand* and *Acumen*. Her fundamental fascination is what makes people tick: how they are affected by early influences in life; how they interrelate; and how they affect one another. She feels reading and writing poetry is a kind of therapy: a communication that facilitates empathy and understanding between people.

CHRISTIAN WARD *p. 79*

Christian Ward is a UK-based writer. Recent work has appeared in *Wild Greens*, *One Hand Clapping*, *Eskimo Pie*, *Literary Yard* and many other publications. While he writes mostly poetry, he occasionally dives into flash fiction.

OYINMIEBI YOUDEOWEI *p. 87*

Oyinmiebi Youdeowei, better known as Miebi, is a fifteen-year-old Nigerian-born writer. She was raised in south-east England and has always loved expressing her creativity in different ways. She recently began writing poetry about various issues in society such as racism, and is happy to begin sharing her work with a larger audience.

---

There were originally another three poems on the shortlist, but sadly we were unable to contact the poets, and therefore couldn't include their poems in this edition.

## SUPPORTERS

This project was made possible through the financial support of the kind people listed below (in alphabetical order).

Rosie Barrett
Zara Branigan
Sharnta Bullard
Chris Cooke
Joanna Cooke
Libby Dady
Matt Dady-Leonard
Rachel Dallaire
Ieva Dapkevicius
Samuel Farrell
Polly Halsey
Ellie Herda-Grimwood
Iain Hood
Celia Hunt
Clémentine Koenig
John Ling
Lizzy Lister
Nuala McGowan
Dana Mills
Kacper Pancewicz
Bella Pearson
Heidi Pyper
Coco van Straaten
Bethany Williams

*and* Anonymous, *on behalf of*
the Grimshaw Girls and their Brother Tom